THE
ARTISAN SODA
Workshop

D1007420

THE
ARTISAN SODA
Workshop

70 Homemade Recipes from Fountain Classics
to Plum Vanilla, Rhubarb Basil, Sea Salt Lime
& Much Much More

Andrea Lynn

 Ulysses Press

Published by:
Ulysses Press
P.O. Box 3440
Berkeley, CA 94703
www.ulyssespress.com

ISBN: 978-1-61243-067-6
Library of Congress Catalog Number 2012937115

Printed in China by Everbest through Four Colour Print Group

10 9 8 7 6 5 4 3 2 1

Acquisitions editor: Keith Riegert
Managing editor: Claire Chun
Editor: Lauren Harrison
Proofreader: Elyce Berrigan-Dunlop
Production: Judith Metzener
Photographs: © www.judiswinksphotography.com except the following from shutterstock.com:
  page 23 © sherrie smith; page 29 © topseller; page 45 © Elena Schweitzer; page 48 © Volosina;
  page 50 © Tim UR; page 76 © Viktar Malyshchyts; page 79 © D7INAMI7S; page 89 © Chiyacat;
  page 99 © matin; page 108 © Lucy Baldwin; page 113 © Valentyn Volkov; page 114 © Scisetti
  Alfio; page 117 © Volosina
Cover design: what!design @ whatweb.com

Distributed by Publishers Group West

To my husband, Ryan, who put up with a refrigerator jam-packed with syrups and graciously tasted and gave feedback on each and every one.

Table of Contents

Fizzy Teas, Floats, and Alcohol-Enhanced Dazzlers 101

Introduction

Soda is one of America's great culinary innovations. Today, Coke and Pepsi are sold around the world. Of course, soda didn't start out as a mass-produced uniform product. A hundred years ago, soda could be enjoyed at local shops that offered it in a wide variety of house-made options. Now, more people are looking back to the history of soda and recognizing all the possibilities; they're applying modern ideas about food to make new and exciting soda recipes. Those who want healthier, fresher, tastier seasonal food are looking for the same in their beverage glass. Artisanal soda makers, like P&H Soda in Brooklyn, are starting to ship their wares across the country. Modern takes on the old-fashioned soda fountain, like the Franklin Foundation in Philadelphia, are starting to sprout up. It's only natural that the next step in the trend is for artisanal soda to find its way into the home kitchen. With a SodaStream (or other seltzer-making device) and a few basic recipes, anyone can make their own delicious sodas.

Soda in America

While carbonation was first invented abroad, America is where sodas first became popular on both small and large scales of production. Carbonated water was originally produced for perceived medicinal benefits, based on the prevalent view that naturally bubbling springs had curative powers. Around the beginning of the nineteenth century, scientists developed processes to use carbon dioxide to carbonate water. In the mid-1800s, carbonated water started to become a popular pharmacy item. Pharmacists soon added a variety of herbs, for both medicinal and flavor purposes.

Pharmacy sodas rose rapidly in popularity. The sodas were claimed to treat a wide array of maladies, and they were particularly popular for their stimulative benefits. Over time, some backlash occurred over concern about the addictive potential of the beverages, particularly those containing cocaine and caffeine. Around the turn of the twentieth century, many pharmacies turned away from the medicinal claims and started advertising sodas based on their sweet fruit flavors.

While pharmacists generally developed their own flavored syrups, some entrepreneurs started selling the pharmacists' most popular blends far and wide. In 1886, Atlanta doctor John Pemberton invented Coca-Cola. The name, derived from the recipe's use of coca leaves and kola nuts, was suggested by Dr. Pemberton's bookkeeper, who also developed the logo's trademark flowing letters. Twelve years later, a North Carolina pharmacist named Caleb Bradham created a popular soda containing pepsin and kola nuts, which was later named Pepsi-Cola.

The beginning of prohibition in 1919 made soda fountains even more popular, as people looked for new places to gather with friends and meet new people. Soon, just about every pharmacy had a soda fountain. Separate ice cream parlors also became widespread, offering ice cream sodas and other carbonated treats.

From the beginning, inventors strove to develop bottling techniques to contain bubbly sodas. By the beginning of the twentieth century, hundreds of bottlers were selling soda to go. Soda six-packs first became available in the 1920s. In the 1950s, aluminum soda cans started to appear on shelves. Over time, the availability of cans and bottles anywhere and everywhere gradually pushed the traditional soda fountains out of existence.

Why Homemade Sodas Are Healthier

Homemade sodas are a bit of work, but the health and flavor benefits are worth the extra effort. Mass-produced store-bought soda is full of chemicals and high-fructose corn syrup. By making homemade soda, you control everything that goes into your beverage, so you know exactly what you're consuming.

Good homemade sodas are made with real fruit, not artificial flavors. Unlike Sunkist, a homemade orange soda contains actual orange. A homemade Sprite can include actual lemon and lime. Using fruit means you're getting added vitamins and antioxidants, helping avoid cancer-causing chemicals.

Another benefit to going homemade is that you can cut down on sugar. Most of the popular sodas in this country are super sweet. If you start experimenting with your own flavors at home, you may find you don't need quite as much sugar as the big companies think. By making sodas to suit your own taste and relying on quality ingredients to add flavor, you'll find that homemade sodas usually have a much lower quantity of sugar while still providing superior taste. With homemade soda recipes, you can also explore the use of alternative sugar sources, like coconut palm sugar and agave syrup, that are better suited to some people's dietary needs. Here's a breakdown of soda sweetener options:

Granulated Sugar   The most popular form of sweetener, granulated sugar (also known as table sugar or sucrose) is refined from sugarcane or sugar beet in a process that originated in India. The raw sugar is processed, crystallized, and dried. While sugarcane and sugar beets bear little resemblance to each other (the former are tall perennial grasses; the latter are tubers), the sugars derived from them are generally considered nutritionally equivalent. Granulated sugar is 50 percent glucose and 50 percent fructose.

Brown Sugar   Molasses is a dark, sweet syrup that's a byproduct of the process of extracting sugar from sugarcane and sugar beets. Brown sugar is table sugar combined with a small amount of molasses, which provides the brown color and deeper, richer flavor. Sugar labeled as "dark brown sugar" simply has a larger percentage of molasses compared to packages labeled "light brown sugar." Most brown sugar is made by adding the molasses back to fully refined sugar, but natural brown sugar (often called "turbinado sugar") is made by only partially refining the sugar, leaving molasses residue intact.

Coconut Palm Sugar   Pure coconut palm sugar is an unrefined natural product made from the nectar of the coconut palm tree. The pure form is available in health food stores, but it's important to check the label because many commercially available brands are blends that mix coconut palm sugar with white cane sugar. Even though it's composed largely of sucrose, it has a lower glycemic index than table sugar. It also contains a variety of vitamins and minerals, which are not present in granulated sugar. Coconut palm sugar has a rich flavor, somewhat similar to brown sugar, but with a more complex taste.

Agave Syrup   Also referred to as agave nectar, this sweetener is derived from the same plant used to make tequila. Sometimes used in place of honey, it has a deep, rich flavor that is about one-and-a-half times sweeter than granulated sugar, which means you can use smaller quantities. It has been touted for its low glycemic index, which makes it a good sweetener for diabetics to use.

Soda vs. Pop vs. Coke

Which term do you use to describe a sweetened carbonated beverage? Soda? Pop? Coke? Soda pop? Soft drink? Your choice probably depends on where you grew up. A study by Matthew Campbell and Prof. Greg Plumb of East Central University in Oklahoma revealed overwhelming regional differences: In the Midwest, it can be referred to as "pop"; in the South, "Coke" is the dominant word of choice; and others in the United States say "soda."

Of course, this wasn't really news. Most of us who have spent time in different areas of the country had already noticed the stark contrasts. As an Alabama-raised girl, I still remember the looks of utter bewilderment when I tried to explain to a bunch of New York friends that I grew up using the word "Coke" to refer to all soft drinks ("Yes, even Sprite!"). It took hours to sort out the confusion. It's clear that Southerners were influenced by the tremendous popularity of Coca-Cola, which originated (and is still headquartered) in Atlanta.

The history of the pop versus soda divide is less obvious. Of course, the two both derive from the term "soda pop," which is rarely used anymore, presumably because it requires a whole second word. "Soda" was the early name for carbonated water because it contained bicarbonate of soda (the name at the time for what we now often refer to as baking soda). The origin of "pop" is still up for debate. Many claim that it refers to the sound made when opening Hutchinson soda bottles that were popular in the 1800s. Others say it's a reference to the beverage's popping bubbles.

Necessary Equipment for Homemade Soda

Here's a list of tools you should have on hand:

Potato Masher   You probably have a potato masher around the house to turn spuds into mashed potatoes. But you probably didn't know it's also a great tool for soda making. For recipes like Kiwi-Strawberry sodas (page 60) or Blackberry-Lavender soda (page 58), the fruit is cooked before being smashed into the syrup mixture. While a fork is an acceptable tool to use, it's much easier to crush the fruit into the liquid with a potato masher.

Fine-Mesh Strainer   Now, I'm sure you have some type of colander or strainer in your kitchen for tasks like draining pasta. But as far as soda-making duties go, you want to make sure to have a fine-mesh strainer. (I like the OXO 8-inch Fine-Mesh Strainer.) The fineness is necessary when you're straining something like a berry syrup. The fine mesh will allow the essence of the fruit to come through, without the skins, seeds, and other solids. Note: If you only have a colander to work with, line it with two layers of cheesecloth to get the same effect as a fine-mesh strainer.

Silicone Spatula   When you put the syrup and fruit concoction into the fine-mesh strainer placed over a bowl, the key to getting all the fruity syrup goodness is a heat-proof silicone spatula. By continually stirring and rotating the spatula in a circular manner, the "mash" of the fruit stays in the strainer, while all the flavor of the syrup drips into the bowl below.

Citrus Reamer   While not absolutely essential, a citrus reamer is a handy tool. A small kitchen utensil used to extract juice from lemons and other citrus fruits, it can also be used to muddle ingredients that require extra stimulation to release their flavors, like those used in Smashed Kumquats with Rosemary Syrup (page 46).

SodaStream   I have a deep love for my SodaStream (www.sodastream.com)—and, no, they're not paying me. If your household uses seltzer on a regular basis, the SodaStream will get a workout and end up being cheaper overall than purchasing seltzer. For the recipes in this book, you can use other soda siphons, or in a pinch, plain old bottled seltzer, but the ease-of-use makes the SodaStream a great product for many households.

The SodaStream uses carbon dioxide cylinders to force the gas into bottles of water. It comes packaged with bottles that are specially designed to be used with the device. It's extremely easy to set up and use and allows the user to adjust the degree of carbonation based on their own taste.

When working with the SodaStream, you carbonate the container of chilled water that the unit comes with. To make flavored soda, you add syrup to the water you've already carbonated. I couldn't understand why I couldn't add the syrup directly into the container with water and then make it into soda. So I went straight to the source. According to SodaStream, "There is a very good reason that only water should be carbonated in your SodaStream home soda maker. You risk damaging your soda maker, not to mention making a big fizzy mess!" Also, the company went onto say that the SodaStream is for carbonating water only. "Be aware that carbonating liquids other than water can be quite dangerous. Sugars in juice, alcohol, milk—even black coffee or tea—can crystallize inside the carbonating tube, causing pressure to build up inside the machine during carbonation." So take it from both me and SodaStream: You want to stick with plain cold water to carbonate and then add flavoring and syrups afterward.

Soda Just the Way You Like It

The recipes in this book aren't scientific formulas, so feel free to adjust as you see fit. The best part of making soda at home is that you're free to make it exactly how you like it. One of the things I like about the SodaStream is that it allows you to adjust the level of carbonation—if you like your soda superfizzy, just use more presses of the machine. Soda syrup quantities can be altered, too. The soda recipes in this book reflect how I like my soda. If you like yours sweeter or bolder, just add more syrup to the seltzer. If you like a soda with just a hint of flavor, add less.

Other Uses for Soda Syrups

While the syrup recipes in this book are primarily intended to make sodas, there's no reason they can't be used in a variety of other ways. Because the flavor is so concentrated, the syrups have the potential to enhance any kind of food that can use a boost of sweetness. Here are some ideas:

- On top pancakes or French toast
- Stirred into oatmeal
- Over ice cream
- As a cocktail mixer
- In a smoothie or milkshake
- Combined with oil and vinegar for a salad dressing

Homemade Soda Copycats

Duplicating soda recipes from the big names in the store-bought world isn't as difficult as you may think. All it takes is the right ingredients cooked into a syrup and mixed with strong seltzer. While store-bought seltzer can certainly be used in a pinch, this is where the SodaStream really comes in handy. For me, the more fruit-based sodas only need two presses of the SodaStream, but for copycat sodas I use three presses for a fizzier drink.

A couple other notes to consider when branching out into the world of copycat soda making: These sodas are made with real ingredients and, while they taste similar to their store-bought counterparts, they're not precise replicas. There are no natural dyes, so in most cases, the colors are more muted. While they can be a little more time-consuming to make than just tossing a bottle of soda into your grocery cart, the flavor more than makes up for the added effort. The Grape Soda is made from reducing Concord grape juice into a syrup. No sugar is even needed for this soda that harnesses all the sweetness and greatness from the grapes. The Cream Soda is flecked with specks of vanilla seeds and has a superior taste to a store-bought drink. Also, these copycat recipes are healthier than the originals in the sense that you're not consuming high-fructose corn syrup or the chemicals of diet sodas.

Natural Golden Cola Syrup

YIELD: ABOUT 1½ CUPS

Have no illusions—this isn't the same thing as cracking open a can of Coke. Instead, this is a homemade soda made from natural ingredients with the same refreshing pucker that you get from Coke. Recipe adapted from Brooklyn Farmacy & Soda Fountain.

Grated zest of 2 medium oranges
Grated zest of 1 large lime
Grated zest of 1 large lemon
½ cinnamon stick
1 star anise pod
½ teaspoon dried lavender flowers
2 teaspoons minced gingerroot
1 vanilla bean, split in half lengthwise
¼ teaspoon citric acid (optional)
2 cups water
1½ cups granulated sugar
1 tablespoon brown sugar

In a medium, heavy pot, combine the orange zest, lime zest, lemon zest, cinnamon stick, star anise, lavender, ginger, vanilla, citric acid, if using, and water. Bring the mixture to a boil over high heat. Reduce the heat to low or medium-low so the mixture is simmering, and let cook for 10 minutes. Remove from the heat and let cool just briefly.

Carefully strain the mixture through a fine-mesh sieve to remove the spices and citrus zest. Return the syrup to the pot, and bring to a boil again over high heat. Add the granulated sugar and brown sugar, and let boil for 5 minutes, stirring to make sure the sugar dissolves. Remove from the heat and let cool. Refrigerate the syrup in a covered container for up to 5 days.

To make Natural Golden Cola: Stir up to ¼ cup Natural Golden Cola Syrup, or to taste, into 8 ounces (1 cup) seltzer.

Dr. Who?: While the jury's out as far as what the 23 ingredients in Dr. Pepper are, adding just a splash of maraschino cherry liquid to the Natural Golden Cola results in a similar taste to the secret formula.

Cherry Cola

YIELD: 1 SERVING

Cherry syrup or maraschino cherry liquid bumps up the cherry-ness of this cola drink.

> ¼ cup Natural Golden Cola Syrup (page 21)
>
> 2 tablespoons jarred maraschino cherry liquid or Cherry-Almond Syrup (page 61)
>
> 8 ounces (1 cup) seltzer

In a glass, stir together the cola syrup and maraschino cherry liquid or cherry-almond syrup to combine. Add the seltzer, stir to combine, and serve.

Orange Syrup

YIELD: ABOUT 1 CUP

Using blood oranges along with navel oranges gives this a deep orange color that's more in tune with an orange soda. While you're juicing, go ahead and include the pulp.

Grated zest and juice of 2 navel oranges
Grated zest and juice of 2 blood oranges
1 tablespoon agave syrup
¼ teaspoon citric acid (optional)

In a nonreactive container, like a 2-cup Mason jar, combine the zest and juice of the navel oranges and the blood oranges. Stir in the agave and citric acid, if using, to combine. Refrigerate in a covered container for 12 to 24 hours. Then, run the syrup through a fine-mesh sieve to remove the zest. Refrigerate the syrup in a covered container for up to 1 week.

To make Orange Soda: Stir up to ¼ cup Orange Syrup, or to taste, into 8 ounces (1 cup) of seltzer.

Helpful Hint: Forget fancy juicers! Gently roll any citrus fruit on a cutting board or countertop to get the most juice possible from the citrus. Cut in half, and then just use old-fashioned clean hands to extract the juices from the citrus.

Cream Soda Syrup

YIELD: ABOUT 1 CUP

One of the easiest soda recipes in the bunch, this is nothing more than vanilla beans, water, and sugar combined to create that crisp, pure vanilla taste of cream soda. This is one time you'll actually want little black specks in your drink—it's just the seeds from the vanilla bean, which add more flavor.

1½ vanilla beans
1 cup water
1¼ cup granulated sugar

Cut the vanilla beans in half lengthwise, and use a knife to scrape the seeds from the bean. Place the vanilla beans and seeds in a medium pot, along with the water and sugar. Bring to a boil over high heat, and boil, stirring occasionally, until the sugar has dissolved, about 2 minutes. Remove from the heat and let cool. Transfer to a covered container and keep the vanilla bean immersed in the syrup so it continues to add flavor. Refrigerate for up to 1 month.

To make Cream Soda: Stir 1½ tablespoons Cream Soda Syrup, or to taste, into 10 ounces (1¼ cups) seltzer.

Helpful Hint: When you've finished making the syrup, don't toss those vanilla beans out. Instead, let them dry at room temperature for a day, then throw them into your container of granulated sugar to lend a little vanilla flavor to it. Or, if you want to get fancy, add the dried vanilla pods to a food processor along with a few cups of granulated sugar to create a very vanilla sweetener.

Ginger Syrup

YIELD: ABOUT 1 CUP

Ginger ale is one of my favorite soda guilty pleasures. But have you ever noticed something missing from it, like a pow of actual ginger? This homemade syrup combines fresh gingerroot and ground ginger for an explosive flavor that's better than any store-bought variety.

2 cups water

1 (6-inch) piece gingerroot, sliced into thin strips

¾ cup granulated sugar

1 tablespoon ground ginger

In a medium pot, combine the water, gingerroot, and sugar. Bring to a boil over high heat, and whisk in the ground ginger. Reduce the heat to medium or medium-low so the mixture is at a simmer. Let cook until the syrup is reduced by half, about 10 minutes. Take off the heat and remove the ginger pieces with either a slotted spoon or by straining the mixture through a fine-mesh sieve. Let the syrup cool, and refrigerate in a covered container for up to 5 days.

To make Ginger Ale: Stir 3 tablespoons Ginger Syrup, or to taste, into 8 ounces (1 cup) seltzer.

Lemon-Lime Syrup

YIELD: ABOUT ¾ CUP

To flavor citrus syrups like this one, the zest is what really gives it that citrus goodness, even more so than the actual juice. But these syrups can't be consumed immediately—they need a stint in the fridge for (preferably) 24 hours.

Grated zest and juice of 3 limes
Grated zest and juice of 2 lemons
1½ tablespoons agave syrup
¼ teaspoon citric acid (optional)

In a nonreactive container, like a 2-cup Mason jar, combine the lime zest and juice, and the lemon zest and juice. Stir in the agave and citric acid, if using, to combine. Refrigerate in a covered container for 12 to 24 hours. Then, run the mixture through a fine-mesh sieve to remove the zest. Refrigerate the syrup in a covered container for up to 1 week.

To make Lemon-Lime Soda: Stir 2 tablespoons Lemon-Lime Syrup, or to taste, into 10 ounces (1¼ cups) seltzer.

Helpful Hint: Citric acid is a white powder extracted from the juice of citrus. Also going by the name "sour salt," this is a tart-tasting seasoning that adds an oomph of extra flavor to some syrups. Find citric acid in supermarkets, health food stores, or online.

Fresca

YIELD: 1 SERVING

Manufactured by Coca-Cola, Fresca is a grapefruit soda drink that has been around since the '50s. This was one of my favorite childhood sodas that I haven't really seen as much as an adult. This homemade Fresca, which combines half fresh grapefruit juice and half seltzer, is even more delicious than its counterpart.

> 1 ruby red grapefruit, halved
> 2 teaspoons agave syrup
> Seltzer, as needed

Juice each grapefruit half, making sure to get the pulp, too. Pour ¾ cup of the juice, including the pulp, into a glass and stir in the agave to combine. Top with seltzer and serve.

Concord Grape Syrup

YIELD: ABOUT ¼ CUP

I salivated at a restaurant after spying Concord grape seltzer on the menu. But the results—a 1 to 3 ratio of Concord grape juice to seltzer—were very disappointing, with the seltzer diluting a majority of the grape flavor. To make a true natural grape soda, you need to take cups of grape juice and boil it down until it makes a syrup consistency. The grapes are sweet enough—no additional sugar needed. Be sure to watch the pot toward the end of the cooking time because it can go from juice to burnt syrup quite rapidly. Yes, this is time-consuming, but the results are worth it, rendering this one of my favorite syrups in the book. For an extra treat, you can stir 1 scoop vanilla ice cream into the grape soda to make a Purple Cow.

2½ cups 100-percent Concord grape juice
1 tablespoon freshly squeezed lemon juice

In a medium, heavy pot, combine the grape juice and lemon juice, and bring to a boil over high heat. Boil until reduced to a syrupy consistency and about ¼ cup of juice remains, 10 to 15 minutes. The mixture will be bubbly, so sometimes it helps to remove the pot from the heat to check the amount. Let cool, and refrigerate in a covered container for up to 5 days.

To make Grape Soda: Stir 2 to 3 teaspoons Concord Grape Syrup, or to taste, into 10 ounces (1¼ cups) seltzer.

PB&J Milkshake

YIELD: 2 SERVINGS

For many, Concord grapes and peanut butter are a beloved flavor combination. This milkshake turns a childhood lunch favorite into a creamy dessert. If you didn't grow up eating grape jelly, feel free to use Strawberry Syrup (page 55) instead.

1 cup vanilla ice cream

½ cup whole milk

3 tablespoons creamy peanut butter

2 tablespoons Concord Grape Syrup (page 31)

In a blender, combine all the ingredients and blend until smooth. Pour into 2 glasses and serve.

Root Beer Syrup

YIELD: ABOUT 2 CUPS

Root beer contains many ingredients, but the most important for its flavoring is sassafras root. However, fresh sassafras is hard to track down due to certain FDA regulations (who knew?), meaning most root beer is made from artificial sassafras flavoring. For this recipe, I chose to use extract for both the sassafras and burdock root, which are easier to find at health food stores than dried root versions.

1 cup water

1 cup brown sugar

1 tablespoon molasses

2 star anise pods

4 cloves

¼ cup sassafras extract

2 tablespoons burdock root extract

In a medium pot, combine the water, brown sugar, molasses, star anise, and cloves. Bring to a boil over high heat, and cook just a few minutes until the sugars dissolve, stirring to combine. Remove from the heat, add the sassafras and burdock root extracts, and stir to combine. Once the liquid is cool, transfer to a container, cover, and refrigerate for a few hours to let the flavors combine. Using a slotted spoon or strainer, remove the star anise and cloves. Refrigerate for up to 2 weeks.

To make Root Beer: Stir up to ¼ cup Root Beer Syrup, or to taste, with 8 ounces (1 cup) seltzer.

Orange-Cream Syrup

YIELD: ABOUT 1½ CUPS

This dreamy drink takes me back to my childhood, sitting on the back porch eating a couple orange Creamsicles (because who can stop with just one?). This magical drink is my re-creation of the classic Popsicle flavor.

> Grated zest of 1 orange
> 2 cups freshly squeezed orange juice or store-bought orange juice with extra pulp
> ½ cup raw cane sugar
> 1½ cups vanilla ice cream

In a medium pot, combine the orange zest and juice, and the sugar. Bring to a boil over high heat, and stir to dissolve the sugar. Let cook until reduced to 1 cup of liquid, 8 to 10 minutes. Remove from the heat, and add the ice cream to the warm liquid to melt. Let cool, and refrigerate in a covered container for up to 3 days.

To make Orange-Cream Soda: Stir ¼ cup Orange-Cream Syrup, or to taste, into 6 ounces (¾ cup) seltzer.

Soda Adventures with Herbs and Spices

Soda syrup beginners will often start out making with simple, straight-forward fruit flavors, but most soda makers will eventually want to add a little sophistication. Herbs and spices can contribute all kinds of bold and subtle flavors to help produce intriguing soda flavor combinations.

Most of the recipes in this chapter pair a sweet fruit with an herb or spice used for complexity and balance. The tropical taste of pineapple matches the slight peppery, minty quality of basil. Mangoes are contrasted by fiery chiles, while plums are complemented by the aromatic flavor of vanilla.

Some herbs and spices, like mint and cinnamon, have a strong enough presence to stand on their own. All the recipes in this chapter produce sodas that are appropriate for a grown-up's palate. These refreshing beverages can be enjoyed on their own, or as a non-alcoholic option with a meal.

Rhubarb-Basil Syrup

YIELD: ¾ CUP

Basil works well with many fruits. Here, it's paired with one of my all-time favorites—rhubarb. For me, the appearance of rhubarb at the farmers' market is one of the first signs of spring, and enjoying a tall rhubarb-basil soda may become a new annual tradition. Don't toss out the cooked rhubarb when you're finished making the syrup. Instead, save it and serve it mixed with yogurt and topped with granola.

4 stalks rhubarb, cut into 1-inch pieces (about 3 cups)
8 to 10 large basil leaves
¾ cup raw cane sugar
1 cup water

In a medium pot, combine the rhubarb, basil leaves, sugar, and water. Bring to a boil over high heat, and stir to dissolve the sugar. Reduce the heat to low or medium-low, and simmer until the rhubarb pieces are completely soft, about 20 minutes. Remove from the heat and let cool. Run the syrup through a fine-mesh sieve to remove the basil and rhubarb, making sure to press the rhubarb against the strainer to extract as much liquid as possible. Refrigerate in a covered container for up to 5 days.

To make Rhubarb-Basil Soda: Stir 2 tablespoons Rhubarb-Basil Syrup, or to taste, into 8 ounces (1 cup) seltzer.

Pineapple-Basil Syrup

YIELD: ½ CUP

The vibrant tropical flavor of pineapple matches well with the hint of basil.

> 2 cups pineapple juice
> 12 to 15 basil leaves

In a medium, heavy pot, combine the pineapple juice and basil leaves, and bring to a boil over high heat. Let boil until reduced to ½ cup, 10 to 15 minutes. Remove from the heat and use a fork to remove the basil leaves from the liquid. Let cool, and refrigerate the syrup in a covered container for up to 5 days.

To make Pineapple-Basil Soda: Stir 2 tablespoons Pineapple-Basil Syrup, or to taste, into 10 ounces (1¼ cups) seltzer.

Kiwi and Juniper Berry Syrup

YIELD: 1 CUP

Juniper berries aren't really berries, but rather plant-produced cones used to flavor gin; they're also incorporated into many Scandinavian dishes. This isn't the prettiest of syrups, but its deliciousness makes up for its looks. The flavor is subtle, which is why the soda has a larger syrup-to-seltzer ratio than other recipes.

4 kiwis, peeled and cut into pieces
¾ cup water
¼ cup coconut palm sugar
1 tablespoon juniper berries

In a medium pot, combine the kiwis, water, sugar, and juniper berries. Bring to a boil over high heat, and stir to dissolve the sugar. Smash the kiwi pieces (which will already be very soft) with a masher. Reduce the heat to low or medium-low, and simmer for 5 minutes. Remove from the heat, and smash the mixture again. Cool to let the juniper flavor infuse the syrup. Run the syrup through a fine-mesh strainer to remove the kiwis and juniper berries. Refrigerate the syrup in a covered container for up to 5 days.

To make Kiwi and Juniper Berry Soda: Stir ¼ cup Kiwi–Juniper Berry Syrup, or to taste, into 6 ounces (¾ cup) seltzer.

Mint Syrup

YIELD: ABOUT 1½ CUPS

When I visited Morocco, every restaurant or store would greet newcomers with a mint tea. Of course, this "exotic" concoction is just mint-soaked hot water that's been heavily sweetened, which appealed to my Southern sweet tea roots. So not only can this syrup be used for a mint soda, but also mixed into hot water for a Moroccan-like mint tea. You can also stir the mint syrup into lemonade or limeade for a refreshing drink on a summer day.

2½ cups roughly chopped mint (include stems and leaves)
¾ cup raw cane sugar
1 cup water

In a medium pot, combine the mint, sugar, and water. Bring to a boil over high heat and stir to dissolve the sugar. Let the mixture boil until the sugar is fully dissolved and the mint is very wilted, for just 1 or 2 more minutes, Remove from the heat. Let cool, then run the syrup through a fine-mesh sieve to remove the mint (discard the leaves). Refrigerate the syrup in a covered container for up to 2 weeks.

To make Mint Soda: Stir ½ tablespoon Mint Syrup, or to taste, into 10 ounces (1¼ cups) seltzer. Garnish with a lime wedge, if desired.

Cinnamon Syrup

YIELD: 1 CUP

A touch of sweetness with a blast of cinnamon makes for a refreshing soda. And when the syrup is finished, I'll reuse the cinnamon sticks by dropping them into a bottle of seltzer water and letting it sit for 12 hours for an oh-so-subtle cinnamon water.

1½ cups water
4 to 5 cinnamon sticks
3 tablespoons agave syrup

In a medium pot, combine the water, cinnamon sticks, and agave. Bring to a boil over high heat, and stir to dissolve the agave. Let boil for 5 minutes, then remove from the heat. Let the syrup cool, leaving the cinnamon sticks in the syrup to continue to flavor it. Refrigerate with the cinnamon sticks in a covered container for up to 2 weeks.

To make Cinnamon Soda: Stir 2 tablespoons Cinnamon Syrup, or to taste, into 10 ounces (1¼ cups) seltzer.

Apricot-Cinnamon Syrup

YIELD: ABOUT ½ CUP

Using dried apricots, this sweet soda can be enjoyed any time of year. The syrup can also be drizzled over ice cream or used as a mixer in a tequila-based drink. After you strain out the apricots, they will be plump and enhanced with cinnamon. For a tasty side dish, chop them up and toss with couscous.

    10 to 12 dried apricots, diced
    ¾ cup water
    ¼ cup brown sugar
    2 cinnamon sticks

In a medium pot, combine the apricots, water, sugar, and cinnamon sticks. Bring to a boil over high heat, and stir to dissolve the sugar. Reduce the heat to medium or medium-low, and simmer until the apricots are plumped and tender, about 10 minutes. Remove from the heat and use a slotted spoon to remove the cinnamon sticks; reserve the cinnamon sticks. Smash the apricots with a masher and let sit for 10 minutes. Using a fine-mesh sieve, remove the fruit from the liquid. Add the cinnamon sticks back into the syrup and let cool. Refrigerate the syrup in a covered container for up to 5 days, leaving the cinnamon sticks in to continue to flavor the syrup.

To make Apricot-Cinnamon Soda: Stir 2 tablespoons Apricot-Cinnamon Syrup, or to taste, into 10 ounces (1¼ cups) seltzer.

Sea Salt–Lime Syrup

YIELD: ABOUT ¾ CUP

Perfect in a margarita, this also makes a simple, refreshing drink on its own. On a hot day, the slightly salty beverage really hits the spot.

½ cup boiling water
½ teaspoon sea salt
1½ tablespoons agave syrup
Grated zest and juice of 2 limes

In a heatproof container, stir together the boiling water and salt to combine. Add the agave and the lime zest and juice, and stir to combine. Let the mixture cool, then refrigerate in a covered container for 12 to 24 hours. Then, strain the mixture through a fine-mesh sieve to remove the lime zest. Refrigerate the syrup in a covered container for up to 7 days.

To make Sea Salt–Lime Soda: Stir 1 tablespoon Sea Salt–Lime Syrup, or to taste, into 10 ounces (1¼ cups) seltzer. If desired, you can even sprinkle a few flakes of sea salt into the glass to serve.

Sparkling Rosemary-Lemonade

YIELD: 1 SERVING

Rosemary adds a little woodsy element to lemonade, which is already a great drink for the outdoors. If you want to turn it into a cocktail, add vodka or gin.

2 tablespoons Rosemary Simple Syrup (page 46)
1½ tablespoons freshly squeezed lemon juice
Seltzer, as needed

In an 8- to 10-ounce glass, stir together the rosemary simple syrup and lemon juice to combine. Top with seltzer. Taste, adjust flavor with additional lemon juice or simple syrup, as needed, and serve.

Smashed Kumquats with Rosemary Syrup

YIELD: 1 SERVING

One of the best ways to make a citrus-based syrup is to use the zest for flavor. Unfortunately, kumquats are virtually impossible to zest because of their miniscule size. Instead, muddle these cute fruits with a rosemary simple syrup to make a drink. This makes a great cocktail, too, if you want to substitute vodka for part of the seltzer. In case you're not familiar with kumquats, note that the entire fruit (except for the seeds) is edible.

ROSEMARY SIMPLE SYRUP

> 2 rosemary sprigs
> ½ cup coconut palm sugar
> ¾ cup water

ROSEMARY-KUMQUAT DRINK

> 4 kumquats
> 1½ tablespoons rosemary simple syrup
> Ice (optional)
> Seltzer, as needed

To make the Rosemary Simple Syrup: Bring the rosemary, sugar, and water to a boil in a medium pot. Boil until fragrant, 3 to 4 minutes. Remove from the heat and let the rosemary steep in the syrup until cool. (You can discard the rosemary once the syrup is cool, but keeping it in the syrup makes the rosemary flavor stronger.) Refrigerate the syrup in a covered container for up to 7 days.

To make the Rosemary-Kumquat Drink: Cut each kumquat in half lengthwise and add them to a glass along with the rosemary simple syrup. Muddle the syrup and kumquats together (a citrus reamer doubles as a great muddler). Add ice, if desired, fill the glass to the top with seltzer, and serve.

Mango-Chile Syrup

YIELD: 1 CUP

A favorite snack of mine is dried or fresh mangoes sprinkled with just a touch of chile powder, which is the inspiration for this soda that delivers a slight walk on the wild side.

2½ cups mango nectar
3 dried red chile pepper pods, halved

In a medium pot, combine the mango nectar and chile pods, and bring to a boil over high heat. Let the mixture boil until reduced to 1 cup, about 10 minutes. (Make sure to keep an eye on the mixture because it will reduce very quickly once the liquid gets low). Remove from the heat and let cool. Strain the pepper pods and seeds from the syrup using a fine-mesh sieve or a slotted spoon. Refrigerate the syrup in a covered container for up to 5 days.

To make Mango-Chile Soda: Stir 2 tablespoons Mango-Chile Syrup, or to taste, into 10 ounces (1¼ cups) seltzer.

Lemon-Thyme Syrup

YIELD: 1 CUP

The pepperiness of thyme matches well with the tartness of lemon in this syrup.

1 cup water
12 thyme sprigs
Grated zest of 2 lemons
¼ cup coconut palm sugar

In a medium pot, combine the water, thyme, lemon zest, and sugar. Bring to a boil over high heat, and let boil until the sugar is completely dissolved and the flavors are gently infused, about 2 minutes. Remove from the heat. Let the syrup cool, leaving the thyme sprigs in to continue to add flavor. Refrigerate in a covered container for up to 2 weeks.

To make Lemon-Thyme Soda: Stir 2 tablespoons Lemon-Thyme Syrup, or to taste, into 10 ounces (1¼ cups) seltzer.

Plum-Vanilla Syrup

YIELD: ABOUT 1 CUP

Plums and vanilla come together for a sweet, tangy, earthy drink. Don't mind the black specks from the vanilla; they add more vanilla flavor.

½ vanilla bean
5 medium-ripe plums, cut into small pieces
1 cup water
⅓ cup coconut palm sugar

Cut the vanilla bean in half lengthwise, and use a knife to scrape the seeds from the bean. In a medium pot, combine the vanilla bean halves and seeds along with the plums, water, and sugar. Bring to a boil over high heat, and stir to dissolve the sugar. Reduce the heat to low or medium-low, and simmer until the plums are soft enough to mash, 10 to 15 minutes. Remove from the heat. Carefully use a fork to remove the vanilla pod, and reserve. Smash the plum pieces into the syrup with a masher. Strain the liquid through a fine-mesh sieve, making sure to press the plum pieces against the strainer to extract as much liquid as possible. Discard the plum pieces (or reserve for another use), and add the vanilla bean back into the syrup to add flavor. Refrigerate the syrup in a covered container for up to 5 days. See page 26 for how to reuse the vanilla bean.

To make Plum-Vanilla Soda: Stir 2 tablespoons Plum-Vanilla Syrup, or to taste, into 8 ounces (1 cup) seltzer.

Lemongrass Syrup

YIELD: 1 CUP

Lemongrass is a stalky plant with a pungent, lemony scent that is commonly used in Thai and Vietnamese cuisine. Lemongrass's medicinal benefits and mild flavor make this soda a mellow, soothing drink.

½ pound lemongrass stalks
¾ cup coconut palm sugar
1½ cups water

Trim the top third of the lemongrass stalks and discard. Chop the remaining lemongrass into 1-inch pieces. In a medium pot, combine the lemongrass, sugar, and water. Bring to a boil over high heat, and stir to dissolve the sugar. Reduce the heat to low or medium-low, and simmer for 20 minutes, so the lemongrass can infuse the syrup. Remove from the heat, and let cool so the lemongrass continues to flavor the syrup. Strain the syrup through a fine-mesh sieve to remove the lemongrass pieces. Refrigerate the syrup in a covered container for up to 7 days.

To make Lemongrass Soda: Stir 2 tablespoons Lemongrass Syrup, or to taste, into 10 ounces (1¼ cups) seltzer.

Cherries
and Berries

Berries quickly became one of my favorite ingredients to work with to make a syrup concentrate. In the peak of summer, you can rely on the sweetest and most flavorful berries, and possibly even decrease the amount of sugar in your recipes. In the winter, you can use the same amount of frozen berries, which have been harvested and flash-frozen at the peak of ripeness. Not only do these drinks have vibrant, glorious colors, they have the taste to match it.

Also, while berries and cherries are great on their own as a soda ingredient, they can also be combined with other fruits and flavors. Strawberries match with the tartness of kiwis, and blueberries are enhanced with a hint of lime. Even better, berries are rich in antioxidants, which help protect our cells from free radicals (translation: they keep our brains and memory strong). Cherries, which are also packed with antioxidants, contain higher levels of melatonin, which aids in sleep, so consider a Cherry-Almond Soda (page 65) before bedtime.

Strawberry Syrup

YIELD: ABOUT 1 CUP

This drink is at its best during the height of summer strawberry season, but you can get pretty good results any time of year. Strawberries are so sweet and delicious, they help make this the perfect drink for turning kids into fans of natural soda. Another great kid-friendly idea: Add 3 tablespoons of syrup to a glass of milk.

1½ cups strawberries, hulled and halved
½ tablespoon freshly squeezed lemon juice
½ cup water
¼ cup raw cane sugar

In a medium pot, combine the strawberries, lemon juice, water, and sugar. Bring to a boil over high heat, and stir to dissolve the sugar. Reduce the heat to medium or medium-low and simmer until the strawberries are very soft, about 10 minutes. When the mixture has simmered for about 5 minutes, smash the strawberries with a masher. When the syrup has finished cooking, remove from the heat and use a fine-mesh sieve to carefully strain the berries from the liquid, making sure to press the fruit against the strainer to extract as much liquid as possible. Discard the strawberries. Refrigerate the syrup in a covered container for up to 5 days.

To make Strawberry Soda: Stir 2 to 3 tablespoons Strawberry Syrup, or to taste, into 10 ounces (1¼ cups) seltzer.

Apple-Cherry Syrup

YIELD: ¾ CUP

This syrup is created by macerating dried cherries in apple juice, and don't you dare throw out these flavorful cherries after the syrup has been made. Instead, toss them into your morning cereal, stir into oatmeal, or bake into chocolate chip cookies.

3 cups apple juice

1 cup dried cherries

1 tablespoon agave syrup

1½ teaspoons freshly squeezed lemon juice

In a medium pot, combine the apple juice and dried cherries. Bring to a boil over high heat, then reduce the heat to medium or medium-low, and simmer until most of the apple juice has reduced, 10 to 15 minutes. There should be about ¾ cup of liquid remaining in the pot. Remove from the heat, and let cool. Use a fine-mesh sieve to strain the cherries from the syrup, making sure to press the cherries against the strainer to extract as much liquid as possible. Stir the agave and lemon juice into the syrup, and cool. Refrigerate the syrup in a covered container for up to 5 days.

To make Apple-Cherry Soda: Stir 3 tablespoons Apple-Cherry Syrup, or to taste, into 8 ounces (1 cup) seltzer.

Hot Buttered Bourbon

YIELD: 1 SERVING

When I have a cold, I like to curl up with a blanket and a hot mug of buttered bourbon. I haven't found a doctor who will sign off on it as a cure, but it comforts me nonetheless. Even if you're feeling well, this is an enjoyable cold-weather drink.

1 tablespoon Apple-Cherry Syrup (page 56)
¼ cup bourbon
Maple syrup or honey (optional)
Boiling water, as needed
1 pat of butter
1 lemon wedge

In a mug, stir the apple-cherry syrup, bourbon, and maple syrup or honey, if using, to combine. Then fill the mug with boiling water, stirring again to combine. Top with a pat of butter to slowly melt in the drink, and serve with a squeeze of lemon.

Blackberry-Lavender Syrup

YIELD: ABOUT 1 CUP

The lavender adds a light botanical flavor to the richness of blackberries. Not only is this a twist on a regular berry soda, but the syrup can also be drizzled on desserts like pound cake or angel food cake.

2 cups blackberries
¾ cup water
¼ cup raw cane sugar
1 teaspoon dried lavender flowers

In a medium pot, combine the blackberries, water, sugar, and lavender. Bring to a boil over high heat, and stir to dissolve the sugar. Reduce the heat to medium or medium-low, and simmer until the berries are completely softened, about 10 minutes. After about 5 minutes, smash the blackberries with a masher. When finished cooking, remove from the heat and let cool. Use a fine-mesh sieve to strain the berries and lavender from the syrup, making sure to press the berries against the strainer to extract as much liquid as possible. Discard the blueberries and lavender. Refrigerate the syrup in a covered container for up to 5 days.

To make Blackberry-Lavender Soda: Stir 2 tablespoons Blackberry-Lavender Syrup, or to taste, into 10 ounces (1¼ cups) seltzer.

Kiwi-Strawberry Syrup

YIELD: ½ CUP

Kiwi and strawberry are a match made in fruit heaven. I first tried the combination in Snapple form, but it's so much better homemade. The tartness of the kiwi perfectly offsets the sweetness of the strawberry.

6 to 8 strawberries, hulled and sliced
2 kiwis, peeled and diced
Freshly squeezed juice of ½ lime
½ cup water
¼ cup sugar

In a medium pot, combine the strawberries, kiwis, lime juice, water, and sugar. Bring to a boil over high heat, and stir to dissolve the sugar. Reduce the heat to medium or medium-low, and simmer until the fruits have softened, about 10 minutes. Remove from the heat, and use a masher to smash the kiwis and strawberries. When cool, use a fine-mesh sieve to strain the fruit from the liquid, making sure to press the fruit against the strainer to extract as much liquid as possible. Refrigerate the syrup in a covered container for up to 5 days.

To make Kiwi-Strawberry Soda: Stir 2 tablespoons Kiwi-Strawberry Syrup, or to taste, into 10 ounces (1¼ cups) seltzer.

Blueberry-Lime Syrup

YIELD: ABOUT 1 CUP

This is an homage to the blueberry-lime jam that my mom used to make when I was a child. The hint of lime enhances the berriness of the blueberries. For a heavenly breakfast, combine this syrup in equal portions with maple syrup, and pour over blueberry pancakes.

1½ cups blueberries
2 tablespoons freshly squeezed lime juice
½ cup water
¼ cup raw cane sugar

In a medium pot, combine the blueberries, lime juice, water, and sugar. Bring to a boil over high heat, and stir to dissolve the sugar. Reduce the heat to medium or medium-low, and simmer until the blueberries are soft and bursting, about 10 minutes. When the mixture has simmered for about 5 minutes, smash the blueberries with a masher. When finished cooking, remove from the heat and use a fine-mesh sieve to carefully strain the blueberries from the liquid, making sure to press the blueberries against the strainer to extract as much liquid as possible. Refrigerate the syrup in a covered container for up to 5 days.

To make Blueberry-Lime Soda: Stir 2 tablespoons Blueberry-Lime Syrup, or to taste, into 10 ounces (1¼ cups) seltzer.

Cranberry, Orange, and Ginger Syrup

YIELD: 1 CUP

I got the idea for this syrup because my much-praised Thanksgiving cranberry sauce includes orange juice and ginger. Tart cranberries plus sweet oranges and a hint of ginger are a winning combo. You can save the smashed cranberries for muffins or other baked goods.

1½ cups fresh or frozen cranberries
2 cups freshly squeezed orange juice
½ cup raw cane sugar
1 (1½-inch) piece gingerroot, peeled and cut into pieces

In a medium pot, combine the cranberries, orange juice, sugar, and ginger. Bring to a boil over high heat, and stir to dissolve the sugar. Reduce the heat to medium, making sure the mixture is at a heavy simmer (but be careful that it doesn't boil over). Cook until the cranberries are soft enough to mash, 10 to 12 minutes. Remove from the heat and carefully smash the cranberries with a masher. Let cool just slightly (too much cooling and the cranberries' high gelatin content kicks in, making it difficult to strain). Then, use a fine-mesh sieve to strain the cranberries and ginger from the syrup, making sure to press the cranberries against the strainer to extract as much liquid as possible. Refrigerate the syrup in a covered container for up to 5 days.

To make Cranberry, Orange, and Ginger Soda: Stir 2 tablespoons Cranberry, Orange, and Ginger Syrup, or to taste, into 10 ounces (1¼ cups) seltzer.

Cherry-Limeade Syrup

YIELD: 1 CUP

Another childhood treat was Sonic's Cherry-Limeade. It's really just a lime soda gussied up with a generous portion of maraschino cherry juice. For some reason, the extra bolt of lime combined with the sweetness of the cherry always called to me. And while I have made my own maraschino cherries, I think the jarred variety better matches the flavor I grew up on.

10 maraschino cherries
½ cup jarred maraschino cherry liquid
Grated zest and juice of 2 limes
1 tablespoon agave syrup

In a nonreactive container, like a 2-cup Mason jar, combine the cherries, cherry liquid, and the lime zest and juice. Muddle the cherries and liquid together. Then, stir in the agave to combine. Cover and refrigerate for 12 to 24 hours. Run the mixture through a fine-mesh sieve to remove the zest and muddled cherries. (This step is optional. Personally, I like the muddled cherries in my drink). Refrigerate the syrup in a covered container for up to 7 days.

To make Cherry-Limeade Soda: Stir 2 tablespoons Cherry-Limeade Syrup, or to taste, into 10 ounces (1¼ cups) seltzer. Garnish with maraschino cherries, if desired.

Cherry-Almond Syrup

YIELD: ABOUT 1 CUP

Pitting cherries is a pain and a half. Instead, cook the cherries whole, then smash them when they're soft. If you're using sour cherries, increase the sugar. Almond extract adds depth to the unadulterated sweetness of cherries, resulting in a syrup that doubles as a pancake topper or tastes great mixed with milk (see sidebar).

> 2 cups sweet cherries
> ¾ cup water
> ⅓ cup raw cane sugar
> 1½ teaspoons almond extract

In a medium pot, combine the cherries, water, and sugar. Bring to a boil over high heat, and stir to dissolve the sugar. Reduce the heat to medium or medium-low so that the liquid is simmering. Let cook until the cherries are soft, about 12 minutes. Remove from the heat, and mash the cherries. When cool, use a fine-mesh sieve to strain the cherries from the liquid, making sure to press the cherries against the strainer to extract as much liquid as possible. Discard the cherries, or save for another use. Add the almond extract to the syrup, stirring to combine. Refrigerate the syrup in a covered container for up to 5 days.

To make Cherry-Almond Soda: Stir 1 to 2 tablespoons Cherry-Almond Syrup, or to taste, into 10 ounces (1¼ cups) seltzer.

Cherry-Almond Milk

YIELD: 1 SERVING

I've enjoyed strawberry milk on occasion, but I've always thought that it's missing something. The cherry-almond syrup has a similar sweetness, but a more complex flavor and a bit of richness that I think makes it a perfect match for milk.

> 2 tablespoons Cherry-Almond Syrup (page 65)
> 8 ounces milk

In an 8- to 10-ounce glass, stir the cherry-almond syrup into a few tablespoons of the milk. Stir well to combine. Top with the remaining milk, stir again, and serve.

Riesling-Raspberry Syrup

YIELD: ½ CUP

Riesling is a relatively sweet white wine native to Germany. For this recipe, make sure the Riesling you purchase is sweet. If you have a drier wine, the amount of sugar may need to be increased to taste. Also, for a stronger raspberry flavor, consider not straining the seeds out (assuming you don't mind seeds in your drink).

- 1½ cups Riesling wine
- 1 cup raspberries
- 2 tablespoons raw cane sugar, plus more as needed

In a medium, heavy pot, combine the wine, raspberries, and sugar. Bring to a boil over high heat, and stir to dissolve the sugar. Reduce the heat to low or medium-low, and simmer until the wine has reduced to about ½ cup, 10 to 15 minutes, making sure to keep an eye on the mixture in the last few minutes (it will reduce very quickly at the end). Let the mixture cool, then use a fine-mesh sieve to strain the raspberries from the syrup, making sure to press the berries against the strainer to extract as much liquid as possible. Refrigerate in a covered container for up to 5 days.

To make Riesling-Raspberry Soda: Stir 2 tablespoons Riesling-Raspberry Syrup, or to taste, into 10 ounces (1¼ cups) seltzer. Proceed with caution with this syrup, as it results in an overload of fizziness.

Helpful Hint: Always be very careful when cooking with alcohol. Use a pot instead of a sauté pan or skillet because if you're cooking over a gas flame, the alcohol can catch fire on the side of a low pan.

Mixed Berry Syrup

YIELD: 1 CUP

Strawberries, blackberries, and blueberries are all great on their own, but when you combine them, the result can be magical. They blend together beautifully in this summer soda. In the winter, a 12-ounce bag of frozen mixed berries can be used instead of fresh. After you strain the cooked berries out of the syrup, try mixing them with yogurt for a smoothie.

1½ cups mixed berries (strawberries, blackberries, and blueberries)
½ cup water
¼ cup raw cane sugar

In a medium pot, combine the mixed berries, water, and sugar. Bring to a boil over high heat, and stir to dissolve the sugar. Reduce the heat to medium or medium-low, and simmer until the berries are soft, 5 to 7 minutes. Remove from the heat and smash the berries with a masher. When the mixture is cool, use a fine-mesh sieve to strain the berries from the liquid, making sure to press the fruit against the strainer to extract as much liquid as possible. Discard the berries, or save for another use. Refrigerate the syrup in a covered container for up to 5 days.

To make Mixed Berry Soda: Stir 2 to 3 tablespoons Mixed Berry Syrup, or to taste, into 10 ounces (1¼ cups) seltzer.

Seasonal
Suds

Making soda with seasonal fruit has two advantages: The fruit's flavor will be at its peak, and making soda is a good way to deal with overabundance. Focusing on what's in season also makes food seem more special because we know the season won't last forever. The recipes in this chapter will take you through the entire calendar, with grapefruits in the winter, rhubarb in the spring, peaches in the summer, and apples in the fall. Also, check out page 122 to learn which seasons are the best for certain sodas.

Here's a simple formula for producing tasty soda: Combine chopped seasonal fruit and a bit of sugar with some fizzy water and add a little ice. The natural sweetness of fruit (sometimes referred to as "nature's candy") makes it the perfect soda ingredient. In many cases, not much more is needed—sometimes you're better off not messing with the basic clarity that nature has produced.

Apple Cider Syrup

YIELD: ½ CUP

Nothing says autumn quite like mulled apple cider. Preblended mulling spices are widely available, or you can make your own blend using cinnamon, nutmeg, cloves, allspice berries, dried citrus peels, and crystallized ginger.

> 3 cups apple cider
> 2 tablespoons mulling spices
> ⅓ cup maple syrup

In a medium, heavy pot, combine the apple cider and mulling spices, and bring to a boil over high heat. Let boil until reduced to ½ cup, 15 to 20 minutes. (As when reducing any juice into a syrup, make sure to watch closely in the last few minutes of cooking to prevent over-reducing and burning.) Add the maple syrup, and stir to combine, then remove the mixture from the heat. Use a fine-mesh sieve to strain out the mulling spices, and let the syrup cool. Refrigerate the syrup in a covered container for up to 5 days.

To make Apple Cider Soda: Stir 2 tablespoons Apple Cider Syrup, or to taste, into 10 ounces (1¼ cups) seltzer.

Grapefruit Syrup

YIELD: ABOUT 1 CUP

The Fresca-inspired soda on page 29 harnesses the sweetness of grapefruit. But real grapefruit lovers enjoy the tangy tartness, which comes through when the syrup is flavored by the zest of the grapefruit like it is here.

> Grated zest of 1 grapefruit
> Juice of 1 grapefruit (about 1 cup)
> 2 tablespoons agave syrup

In a nonreactive container, like a 2-cup Mason jar, combine the grapefruit zest and juice. Stir in the agave to combine. Refrigerate for 12 to 24 hours. Then, run the syrup through a fine-mesh sieve to remove the zest. Refrigerate the syrup in a covered container for up to 7 days.

To make Grapefruit Soda: Stir 2 tablespoons Grapefruit Syrup, or to taste, into 10 ounces (1¼ cups) seltzer.

Peach Syrup

YIELD: ½ CUP

This is a subtle syrup with a mild peachiness lurking in the background. If you're making this syrup in the winter, consider using frozen peaches, which will have been frozen at the fruit's peak ripeness.

2 cups sliced peaches or 1 (16-ounce) bag frozen peaches, thawed
½ cup water
¼ cup raw cane sugar

In a medium pot, combine the peaches, water, and sugar. Bring to a boil over high heat, and stir to dissolve the sugar. Reduce the heat to medium or medium-low, and simmer until the peaches are tender, about 10 minutes. Remove from the heat, and smash the peach slices with a masher. When cool, use a fine-mesh sieve to strain the fruit from the liquid, making sure to press the fruit against the strainer to extract as much liquid as possible. Refrigerate the syrup in a covered container for up to 5 days.

To make Peach Soda: Stir 2 to 3 tablespoons Peach Syrup, or to taste, into 10 ounces (1¼ cups) seltzer.

Very Plum Syrup

YIELD: ABOUT 1 CUP

Prune juice isn't a particularly sexy ingredient, but the resulting plum soda is a sophisticated beverage with a subtle sweetness and an earthy flavor. Don't throw out the strained plums when you're done; they make a fantastic topping for yogurt or vanilla ice cream (or baked into a cake or other sweets).

4 plums, pitted and diced into medium pieces, or 8 to 10 prunes

1 cup prune juice

¼ cup raw cane sugar

In a medium pot, combine the plums or prunes, prune juice, and sugar. Bring to a boil over high heat, and stir to dissolve the sugar. Reduce the heat to medium or medium-low, and simmer until the plum pieces or prunes are soft, about 10 minutes. Remove from the heat, and smash the plums or prunes with a masher. Let cool, then use a fine-mesh sieve to remove the plums or prunes from the liquid, making sure to press the fruit against the strainer to extract as much liquid as possible. Refrigerate the syrup in a covered container for up to 5 days.

To make Very Plum Soda: Stir 2 tablespoons Very Plum Syrup, or to taste, into 10 ounces (1¼ cups) seltzer.

Pineapple Syrup

YIELD: 1 CUP

As the pineapple juice boils down for this tropical syrup, the juice turns even sweeter, so very little additional sweetener is needed. Use this syrup to make the Creamy Piña Colada on page 118 or just top with coconut milk for a non-alcoholic drink.

> 3 cups pineapple juice
> 1 tablespoon agave syrup

In a medium, heavy pot, bring the pineapple juice to a boil over high heat. Let boil until reduced into about 1 cup that has a syrupy consistency, 10 to 15 minutes. The mixture will be bubbly and syrupy, so sometimes it helps to remove from the heat to see the true amount. When reduced, remove from the heat, stir in the agave, and allow to cool. Refrigerate in a covered container for up to 5 days.

To make Pineapple Soda: Stir 1½ to 2 tablespoons Pineapple Syrup, or to taste, into 10 ounces (1¼ cups) seltzer.

Rhubarb-Grapefruit Syrup

YIELD: ABOUT 2 CUPS

This drink brings two of my favorite flavors together for an unusual (and unusually delicious) combination.

> 1 pound rhubarb, cut into 1-inch pieces
> Juice of 2 grapefruits (about 1½ cups)
> ½ cup agave syrup

In a large pot, combine the rhubarb pieces, grapefruit juice, and agave. Bring to a boil over high heat, and stir to combine the agave with the mixture. Reduce the heat to low or medium-low, and simmer until the rhubarb is soft, about 15 minutes. Remove from the heat. Using a masher, smash the rhubarb into the liquid mixture. Let cool. Then, use a fine-mesh sieve to strain the liquid, making sure to press the fruit against the fine-mesh strainer to extract as much liquid as possible. Discard the rhubarb pieces, or save for another use. Refrigerate the syrup in a covered container for up to 5 days.

To make Rhubarb-Grapefruit Soda: Stir ¼ cup Rhubarb-Grapefruit Syrup, or to taste, into 8 ounces (1 cup) seltzer.

Prickly Pear Syrup

YIELD: ½ CUP

Prickly pear is the fruit of a paddle-shaped cactus. Some people describe its flavor as reminiscent of bubblegum. Don't be intimidated; it's easier to work with prickly pears than it seems. The soda's magenta hue makes this one the most beautiful of the bunch.

> 8 prickly pears
> 3 cups water
> 2 tablespoons agave syrup

To tackle the prickly pear, use a cutting board that you don't mind potentially staining. Slice off both ends of each prickly pear. Then, cut down one side of the prickly pear skin. Use your hands to open the skin around the prickly pear and remove the flesh. You can use your hands to break the flesh into pieces, or chop with a knife.

Combine the prickly pear pieces and the water in a medium pot. Bring to a boil over high heat. Reduce the heat to low or medium-low, and let simmer for about 15 minutes, until most of the liquid is gone, with just ½ cup remaining, plus the prickly pear seeds. Remove from the heat, and let cool. Use a fine-mesh sieve to strain the pulp and seeds from the syrup, making sure to press it against the strainer to extract as much liquid as possible. Stir in the agave to combine. Refrigerate the syrup in a covered container for up to 5 days.

To make Prickly Pear Soda: Stir 2 tablespoons Prickly Pear Syrup, or to taste, into 10 ounces (1¼ cups) seltzer.

Pear, Grape, and Honey Syrup

YIELD: ABOUT 1 CUP

This syrup produces a rich, sweet autumn soda, mingling the lushness of grapes with the sweet goodness of pears. I also enjoy a drizzle of this syrup in a snifter of brandy.

1½ cups chopped Bartlett pears (about 2 medium)
1 cup grape juice
¼ cup honey

Combine the pears and grape juice in a medium pot. Bring to a boil over high heat. Reduce the heat to medium or medium-low, and simmer until the pears are soft, about 10 minutes. Add the honey and stir to combine. Remove from the heat, and use a masher to smash the pears. Let cool, then use a fine-mesh sieve to strain the pears from the liquid, making sure to press the fruit against the strainer to extract as much liquid as possible. Refrigerate in a covered container for up to 5 days.

To make Pear, Grape, and Honey Soda: Stir 2 tablespoons Honey, Grape, and Pear Syrup, or to taste, into 10 ounces (1¼ cups) seltzer.

Carrot-Maple Syrup

YIELD: 1 CUP

As the carrot juice is reduced into a syrup consistency, the sweetness of the carrots intensifies. This dark orange syrup produces a deliciously sweet soda.

2½ cups carrot juice
1½ tablespoons maple syrup
2 teaspoons freshly squeezed lemon juice

In a medium pot, bring the carrot juice to a boil over high heat. Let boil until reduced to 1 cup, 10 to 15 minutes. (Make sure to keep an eye on the carrot juice because it will reduce very quickly once the liquid gets low.) Stir in the maple syrup to combine, and remove from the heat. Stir in the lemon juice. Refrigerate in a covered container for up to 5 days.

To make Carrot-Maple Soda: Add 3 tablespoons Carrot-Maple Syrup into a few tablespoons of seltzer. Stir vigorously to combine (the syrup is very thick). Then, fill the glass with seltzer, about 6 ounces (¾ cup).

Tomato Water

YIELD: ABOUT 2 CUPS

Tomato water, which was trendy way back in the '90s, has lots of uses, from a Bloody Mary ingredient to sauce for fish. For the true tomato lover, there's something to be said for adding a little seltzer and just basking in the tomato aroma and flavor. The salt is used to help draw out the juices from the tomatoes. The yield for this recipe will depend on the juiciness of the tomatoes, so aim for very ripe ones. Don't toss out the chopped tomatoes when the juices have been extracted. Instead, mix the tomatoes with 1 teaspoon minced garlic, 1½ cups Greek yogurt, ½ teaspoon salt, and 1 peeled and chopped cucumber. Purée, and you have a gazpacho.

  2 pounds ripe tomatoes, chopped
  1½ teaspoons kosher salt

Place a sieve or a colander lined with one layer of cheesecloth in a large pot. Add the chopped tomatoes and salt. Briefly toss to combine. Cover the pot and refrigerate overnight.

Remove from the fridge and, using clean hands or wearing gloves, squeeze the tomato pieces to extract more liquid. Then, use a spatula to press the tomato pieces against the strainer to extract as much liquid as possible. (Save the tomato pieces for another use, like making gazpacho). Refrigerate the syrup in a covered container for up to 3 days.

To make Fizzy Tomato Water: Add 1 cup tomato water to a glass. Top with 2 ounces (¼ cup) seltzer. Garnish with a lemon wedge, if desired.

Pomegranate-Lime Syrup

YIELD: ABOUT 1 CUP

Full of antioxidants, pomegranate juice has a beautiful flavor and color. This invigorating soda is a great way to get a boost any time of day.

2½ cups pomegranate juice
¼ cup raw cane sugar
Juice of ½ lime

In a medium pot, combine the pomegranate juice and sugar. Bring to a boil over high heat, and stir to dissolve the sugar. Let the liquid reduce to 1 cup, 12 to 15 minutes. Be careful to keep a close eye on the mixture toward the last few minutes, so it doesn't over-reduce. Remove from the heat, and stir in the lime juice. Refrigerate in a covered container for up to 5 days.

To make Pomegranate-Lime Soda: Stir 1 to 2 tablespoons Pomegranate-Lime Syrup, or to taste, into 8 ounces (1 cup) seltzer.

Banana–Brown Sugar Syrup

YIELD: ½ CUP

The riper the banana, the less need for sugar. Beware that cooking this syrup will have your kitchen smelling like banana bread and make you crave it (or is that just me?).

3 medium, ripe bananas, peeled and cut into 1-inch pieces
¾ cup water
2 tablespoons brown sugar

In a medium pot, combine the banana pieces, water, and brown sugar. Bring to a boil over high heat, and stir to dissolve the sugar. Reduce the heat to medium or medium-low, and simmer until the bananas are soft, about 5 minutes. Remove from the heat and smash the bananas with a masher. Once the syrup has cooled, use a fine-mesh sieve to strain the banana mash from the liquid, making sure to press the fruit against the strainer to extract as much liquid as possible. Save the banana to use in a smoothie, if desired. Refrigerate the syrup in a covered container for up to 5 days.

To make Banana–Brown Sugar Soda: Stir 2 tablespoons Banana-Brown Sugar Syrup, or to taste, into 10 ounces (1¼ cups) seltzer.

Agua Frescas
and Shrubs

While exploring the world of homemade sodas, I found there's a wide, wide world of other sparkling beverages that go beyond fruit concentrates.

The first are fizzy agua frescas. These came about after I discovered that watery fruits, like melons, are best used in a carbonated beverage when they are puréed and strained, as opposed to being reduced into a syrup. The results struck me as being very similar to an agua fresca. Translated as "fresh water," these are fresh fruit drinks popular in Mexico and traditionally made from a combination of fresh fruit, water, and sugar. All kinds of fruits are used in agua frescas, but some of the most popular flavors involve melons.

Another quite different type of sparkler is a shrub. All the rage back in the colonial days, shrubs are gradually becoming more popular as a cocktail component, but another great use for them is as a soda ingredient. Shrubs got their start in the eighteenth century when vinegar was used to prevent fruit from spoiling. Vinegar, fruit, sugar, and water were combined to create beverages that didn't require refrigeration. Shrubs weren't merely practical; the tart and sweet mix is a bracing flavor combination. While the idea of a vinegar beverage sounds a tad odd to a lot of people, it's really quite refreshing. Vinegar helps ready the taste buds and highlight the flavor of the fruit it's paired with.

Fizzy Cantaloupe Agua Fresca

YIELD: ABOUT 1¾ CUPS

My husband still raves about the cantaloupe agua fresca he enjoyed in San Francisco's Mission District over six years ago. I can't eat a cantaloupe without hearing about that agua fresca, so I had to create one to rival his discovery from years before.

CANTALOUPE JUICE

2½ cups cubed cantaloupe

1 tablespoon agave syrup

2 teaspoons freshly squeezed lemon juice

In a food processor or blender, combine the cantaloupe, agave, and lime juice. Blend until all the cantaloupe is puréed, 1 to 2 minutes. Then, fit a bowl with a fine-mesh sieve, and pour the juice through the strainer to catch the pulp. Make sure to press the puréed fruit against the strainer to extract as much liquid as possible, and discard the pulp. Refrigerate the cantaloupe juice in a covered container for up to 3 days.

To make Fizzy Cantaloupe Agua Fresca: Fill a 10-ounce glass with 8 ounces (1 cup) cantaloupe juice. Top with seltzer, and serve.

Fizzy Watermelon-Jalapeño Agua Fresca

YIELD: ABOUT 2 CUPS

Watermelon and jalapeño make for a great pairing of sweet and heat. The level of heat in individual jalapeños can vary quite a bit, so you may want to taste as you go to get a sense of the spice level. Jalapeño seeds contain a lot of the pepper's punch, so make sure to include them.

JALAPEÑO SIMPLE SYRUP

- 1 jalapeño, chopped, seeds included
- ½ cup water
- ½ cup granulated sugar

WATERMELON JUICE

- 2½ cups cubed watermelon
- 2 teaspoons freshly squeezed lime juice

To make the simple syrup: In a small pot, combine the jalapeño, water, and sugar. Bring to a boil over high heat and then let cook until the sugar is entirely dissolved and the syrup is flavored with jalapeño, 2 to 3 minutes. Remove from the heat and let cool. Then, use a fine-mesh sieve to strain the jalapeño pieces out of the simple syrup. Refrigerate the syrup in a covered container for up to 7 days.

To make the watermelon juice: In a food processor or blender, combine the watermelon and lime juice. Blend until all the watermelon is puréed, 1 to 2 minutes. Then, fit a bowl with a fine-mesh sieve, and pour the juice through strainer to catch the pulp. Make sure to press the puréed fruit against the strainer to extract as much liquid as possible, and discard the pulp. Refrigerate the watermelon juice in an airtight container for up to 3 days.

To make Fizzy Watermelon-Jalapeño Agua Fresca: Fill a 10-ounce glass with 8 ounces (1 cup) watermelon juice. Stir in 1 to 2 teaspoons of jalapeño simple syrup to taste. Top with seltzer, and serve.

Fizzy Cucumber-Mint Agua Fresca

YIELD: ABOUT 2 CUPS

This is the perfect drink for someone who wants a flavorful refreshment but doesn't have a big sweet tooth. Cucumber and mint come together for a cool, brightly flavored drink.

CUCUMBER-MINT JUICE
> 2 medium cucumbers, peeled and cut into 1-inch pieces
> 1 tablespoon freshly squeezed lemon juice
> 1 tablespoon Mint Syrup (page 41)

In a food processor or blender, combine the cucumber pieces, lemon juice, and mint syrup. Blend until all the cucumber is puréed, 1 to 2 minutes. Then, fit a bowl with a fine-mesh sieve, and pour the juice through the strainer to catch the pulp. Make sure to press the puréed cucumber against the strainer to extract as much liquid as possible, and discard the pulp. Refrigerate the juice for up to 3 days.

To make Fizzy Cucumber-Mint Agua Fresca: Fill a 10-ounce glass with 8 ounces (1 cup) cucumber juice, top with seltzer, and serve.

Fizzy Honeydew-Strawberry Agua Fresca

YIELD: ABOUT 1¼ CUPS

Honeydews are considered by many to be the sweetest melons. The strawberries add flavor and a bit of thickness to this refreshing agua fresca.

HONEYDEW-STRAWBERRY JUICE

    2 cups cubed honeydew melon

    ¼ cup sliced strawberries

    1 tablespoon honey

    2 teaspoons lime juice

In a food processor or blender, combine the honeydew, strawberries, honey, and lime juice. Blend until all the fruit is puréed, 1 to 2 minutes. Then, fit a bowl with a fine-mesh sieve, and pour the juice through the strainer to catch the pulp. Make sure to press the puréed fruit against the strainer to extract as much liquid as possible, and discard the pulp. Refrigerate the juice for up to 3 days.

To make Fizzy Honeydew-Strawberry Agua Fresca: Fill a 10-ounce glass with 8 ounces (1 cup) honeydew-strawberry juice. Top with seltzer, and serve.

Fizzy Papaya-Orange Agua Fresca

YIELD: ABOUT 2 CUPS

This drink has a fairly intense papaya flavor, so make sure you are on board with the sweet richness of papaya before making this recipe. If you can find blood oranges, use their juice instead of navel orange juice for a more intense orange color and flavor.

PAPAYA-ORANGE JUICE

　2 cups cubed papaya

　1½ tablespoons agave syrup

　½ cup freshly squeezed orange juice

In a food processor or blender, combine the papaya and agave. Blend until all the papaya is puréed, 1 to 2 minutes. Then, fit a bowl with a fine-mesh sieve, and pour the juice through the strainer to catch the pulp. Make sure to press the puréed papaya against the strainer to extract as much liquid as possible, and discard the pulp. Stir in the orange juice, and refrigerate in a covered container for up to 3 days.

To make Fizzy Papaya-Orange Agua Fresca: Fill a 10-ounce glass with 8 ounces (1 cup) papaya-orange juice. Top with seltzer, and serve.

Plum Shrub

YIELD: ABOUT 1 CUP

This is a great place to start your appreciation of shrubs. While the drink has the distinct vinegar clarity you expect from shrubs, a strong plum flavor also comes through. Note that the riper the fruit is, the less sugar you'll need.

> 1 cup chopped ripe plums (about 2)
>
> 1 cup apple cider vinegar, or more as needed, like Bragg's Organic Apple Cider Vinegar
>
> ⅓ cup raw cane sugar

In a nonreactive container, like a 2-cup Mason jar, place the chopped plums. Top with the vinegar, making sure the fruit is entirely covered (and adding more vinegar, if needed). Cover the mixture, and let sit at room temperature for 5 days, shaking the container once a day.

When the mixture is ready, transfer the liquid and fruit to a medium pot. Add the sugar, and bring to a boil over high heat. Let boil for about 5 minutes, stirring to make sure the sugar is dissolved, and smashing the plum pieces into the liquid. Remove from the heat, and let cool. Use a fine-mesh sieve to strain the fruit from the shrub, and transfer the liquid to a covered container. Refrigerate for up to 2 weeks.

To serve, stir 3 tablespoons Plum Shrub, or to taste, into 8 ounces (1 cup) seltzer.

Grape Shrub

YIELD: ABOUT 1 CUP

Grape juice is extremely sweet, but this shrub strips that down a bit, revealing a clearer essence of grape flavor. You'll want to boil the vinegar until the grapes are soft, but make sure to keep an eye on it. You don't want all of the vinegar's hard work to boil down.

1 cup red seedless grapes, halved

1 cup apple cider vinegar, or more as needed, like Bragg's Organic Apple Cider Vinegar

⅓ cup raw cane sugar

In a nonreactive container, like a 2-cup Mason jar, place the chopped grapes. Top with the vinegar, making sure the fruit is entirely covered (and adding more vinegar, if needed). Cover the mixture, and let sit at room temperature for 5 days, shaking the container once a day.

When the mixture is ready, transfer the liquid and fruit to a medium pot. Add the sugar, and bring to a boil over high heat. Let boil for about 5 minutes, stirring to make sure the sugar is dissolved, and smashing the grapes into the liquid. Remove from the heat, and let cool. Use a fine-mesh sieve to strain the fruit from the shrub, and transfer the liquid to a covered container. Refrigerate for up to 2 weeks.

To serve, stir 3 tablespoons Grape Shrub, or to taste, into 8 ounces (1 cup) seltzer.

Strawberry-Balsamic Shrub

YIELD: ABOUT 1 CUP

Strawberries and balsamic are a favorite combination of mine. The slightly sweet, rich flavor of balsamic makes it a great addition to a strawberry dessert. In soda form, the combination produces a lovely depth of flavor.

1 cup hulled, chopped strawberries

½ cup balsamic vinegar

1 cup apple cider vinegar, or more as needed, like Bragg's Organic Apple Cider Vinegar

⅓ cup raw cane sugar

In a nonreactive container, like a 2-cup Mason jar, place the strawberries. Top with the balsamic vinegar and apple cider vinegar, making sure the fruit is entirely covered (and adding more apple cider vinegar, if needed). Cover the mixture, and let sit at room temperature for 5 days, shaking the container once a day.

When the mixture is ready, transfer the liquid and fruit to a medium pot. Add the sugar, and bring to a boil over high heat. Let boil for about 5 minutes, stirring to make sure the sugar is dissolved, and smashing the strawberries into the liquid. Remove from the heat, and let cool. Use a fine-mesh sieve to strain the fruit from the shrub, and transfer the liquid to a covered container. Refrigerate for up to 2 weeks.

To serve, stir 3 tablespoons Strawberry-Balsamic Shrub, or to taste, into 8 ounces (1 cup) seltzer.

Persimmon–Black Pepper Shrub

YIELD: ABOUT 1 CUP

Persimmons are an Asian fruit with a deep orange color and a floral taste, which is nicely contrasted by black pepper in this recipe. The peppercorns need to be cracked to ensure that the flavor absorbs into the persimmon vinegar. To do this, seal the 2 teaspoons of black peppercorns into a zip-top bag. Then, gently whack them with the back of a saucepan or a rolling pin to crack them. This shrub makes an excellent cocktail when mixed with cognac or brandy.

1 cup chopped Fuyu persimmons

2 teaspoons cracked black peppercorns (see note above)

1 cup apple cider vinegar, or as needed, like Bragg's Organic Apple Cider Vinegar

⅓ cup raw cane sugar

The Perfect Shrub

A properly conceived shrub soda should have the perfect balance of fruit flavor, sweetness, and tartness. I find the tartness is best achieved with apple cider vinegar, especially Bragg's Organic Apple Cider Vinegar because it's unpasteurized and contains living nutrients and bacteria. Also note that the sweetness of the shrub could depend on the ripeness of the fruits used. If more sweetness is needed to create the trifecta of acid, fruit, and sweetness, just stir a little agave syrup into the final product.

In a nonreactive container, like a 2-cup Mason jar, combine the chopped persimmons and peppercorns. Top with the vinegar, making sure the fruit is entirely covered (and adding more vinegar, if needed). Cover the mixture, and let sit at room temperature for 5 to 7 days, shaking the container once a day.

When the mixture is ready, transfer the liquid and fruit to a medium pot. Add the sugar, and bring to a boil over high heat. Let boil for about 5 minutes, stirring to make sure the sugar is dissolved, and smashing the persimmons as best you can into the liquid. Remove from the heat, and let cool. Use a fine-mesh sieve to strain the fruit from the shrub, and transfer the liquid to a covered container. Refrigerate for up to 2 weeks.

To serve, stir 3 tablespoons of Persimmon–Black Pepper Shrub, or to taste, into 8 ounces (1 cup) seltzer.

Quickie Pear Shrub

YIELD: 1 CUP

Don't have the time to make a real shrub? Not totally sold that you're going to like them? Try this fast and easy shrub to get a feel for the vinegar beverage.

½ cup pear juice or nectar

1 tablespoon apple cider vinegar, like Bragg's Organic Apple Cider Vinegar

3 tablespoons agave syrup

In a small bowl, stir together the pear juice or nectar, vinegar, and agave to combine.

To serve, stir 3 tablespoons Quickie Pear Shrub, or to taste, into 8 ounces (1 cup) seltzer.

Fizzy Teas, Floats, and Alcohol-Enhanced Dazzlers

Once you start carbonating beverages, you realize there's no reason to stop with the basics. All kinds of things work well in sodas: herbal infusions, teas, even coffee and chocolate. If you can drink it, you can carbonate it.

And when your kitchen is full of soda syrups (like mine was), you realize that there is an almost infinite number of uses for them. The concentrated flavor can be unleashed in any kind of drink. Syrups are particularly useful in dairy-based dessert drinks, like floats, where the strong syrup flavors stand up to the dairy. Check out the Coffee Soda Float (page 107), which can compete with any Starbucks creation, without the price tag. The same holds true for cocktails, where a strong alcohol can stand toe-to-toe with an intensely flavorful syrup, like in the Kahlúa Egg Cream (page 112). Many of the syrup recipes in this book can be utilized to create bold flavors at your next cocktail party.

Green Tea Syrup

YIELD: ABOUT 1 CUP

Green tea is the least-processed type of tea, which is why it has the most antioxidants. It has been used for medicinal purposes for over 4,000 years. Studies have shown that green tea can help prevent cancer, heart disease, and weight gain. So, what are you waiting for? If you haven't managed to work a hot cup into your daily routine, this mild soda might be the perfect way to improve your health.

> 1 cup boiling water
> 2 tablespoons honey
> 5 bags green tea

In a heatproof container, stir together the boiling water and honey to combine. Add the tea bags, and steep the tea for 10 minutes. Remove the tea bags, and let cool. Refrigerate in a covered container for up to 5 days.

To make Green Tea Soda: Stir 2 tablespoons Green Tea Syrup, or to taste, into 10 ounces (1¼ cups) seltzer.

Hibiscus Syrup

YIELD: 1 CUP

It's not just that I enjoy the floral, tart taste of hibiscus. Even better, dried hibiscus flowers are ultrahigh in vitamin C and minerals, and they promote a number of other nutritional benefits. For a festive sparkling cocktail, add 1 tablespoon Hibiscus Syrup to 4 ounces champagne or other sparkling wine.

1 cup water

3 tablespoons honey

8 hibiscus tea bags (I enjoy Republic of Tea brand) or 3 tablespoons loose dried hibiscus

In a small pot, bring the water to a boil over high heat. Once boiling, remove from the heat and stir in the honey. Add the tea bags or loose hibiscus and let steep for 15 minutes. Then, either remove the tea bags or use a fine-mesh sieve to strain out the loose hibiscus. Taste, and add additional honey, if needed. Let cool, and refrigerate the syrup in a covered container for up to 3 days.

To make Hibiscus Soda: Stir 2 tablespoons Hibiscus Syrup, or to taste, into 10 ounces (1¼ cups) seltzer.

Coffee Concentrate

YIELD: 2 SERVINGS

Cold-brewing is the best way to make iced coffee. While I was initially intrigued by the process because of the novelty (you can brew coffee without heat!), I quickly discovered that it has actual advantages. Cold-brewing greatly reduces coffee's bitterness, allowing other flavors to gain much greater prominence. While it sounds time-consuming, it's really pretty simple to let the coffee brew overnight.

6 tablespoons drip-ground coffee
1½ cups water

Stir together the ground coffee and water in a container or large glass (or a French press if you have one). After 10 minutes, stir the coffee again to make sure the grounds are all immersed in water. Cover the container with plastic wrap and let sit at room temperature for 12 hours.

After 12 hours, pour the mixture once through a fine-mesh sieve to capture the coffee grounds. Then, slowly strain it a second time through cheesecloth to capture the smaller pieces of sediment. (If you have a French press, you can use it to strain the coffee.)

To make Cold-Brewed Coffee: Fill a glass with ice and add ½ cup coffee concentrate and ½ cup cold water.

Coffee Soda Float

YIELD: 1 SERVING

This coffee soda float is like a rustic Frappuccino—it's a great mid-day treat. The undiluted cold-brewed coffee is a great base for this beverage for two reasons: Its less-bitter taste makes it a great option for cold coffee drinks, and its concentrated strength means that you won't have a weak cup after you add the seltzer. For an added punch, consider adding just a hint of Bailey's Irish Cream to the float.

½ cup Coffee Concentrate (page 106)

1 teaspoon agave syrup

2 heaping tablespoons vanilla ice cream, thawed at room temperature

4 to 6 ounces seltzer

In a tall glass, stir the coffee concentrate and agave together to combine. Add the vanilla ice cream, and stir to combine. Top with the seltzer, and gently stir to combine. Serve.

Bourbon Root Beer Float

YIELD: 1 SERVING

While cooking ribs glazed in root beer and bourbon, I had the inspiration to bring these two American classics together in an adult beverage that will remind you of your childhood.

    6 ounces Root Beer (page 33)
    2 ounces bourbon
    2 heaping tablespoons vanilla ice cream
    Whipped cream (optional)

In a 10-ounce glass, stir together the root beer and bourbon to combine. Top with the ice cream, gently stirring once or twice. If desired, top with a dollop of whipped cream.

Chocolate Syrup

YIELD: ABOUT ¾ CUP

I'm not sure why chocolate soda isn't more popular—I was surprised by how much I enjoyed (and occasionally craved) this drink. A glass is chocolatey enough to fill in for dessert while being relatively low in fat and calories. If you're questioning the need to make chocolate syrup instead of just using a store-bought bottle, trust me and try it. Homemade syrup tastes much more like chocolate and much less like chemicals than what you get in a plastic bottle. Use this chocolate syrup to also make an Egg Cream (page 110). Or, to make a chocolate-mocha syrup, just add 1 tablespoon espresso instant coffee, like my favorite, Medaglia D'Oro Instant Espresso, into the pot along with the cocoa.

   ¾ cup water
   ⅓ cup good-quality natural-process unsweetened cocoa powder
   ¼ cup raw cane sugar
   1 tablespoon vanilla extract

In a medium, heavy pot, combine the water, cocoa powder, sugar, and vanilla extract. Bring to a boil over high heat, and let boil until thickened, 2 to 4 minutes, whisking vigorously to combine. Remove from the heat, and let cool. Refrigerate in a covered container for up to 7 days.

To make Chocolate Soda: Stir 2 tablespoons Chocolate Syrup, or to taste, into 10 ounces (1¼ cups) seltzer.

Egg Cream

YIELD: 1 SERVING

Egg creams are a classic old-time New York concoction made with milk, seltzer, and chocolate syrup. Traditionalists may balk at my use of cream instead of milk, but I think using a smaller volume of richer dairy results in more seltzer, and thus a fizzier beverage. Traditionalists suggest serving a pretzel rod with the egg cream.

1½ tablespoons cream
2 tablespoons Chocolate Syrup (page 109)
¾ cup seltzer

In a 10- to 12-ounce glass, stir together the cream and chocolate syrup to thoroughly combine. Slowly pour in the seltzer. Gently stir again if needed.

Kahlúa Egg Cream

YIELD: 1 SERVING

I think this adult egg cream is a fun final course at a casual dinner party. It's both a dessert and a mild cocktail. If your crowd wants a stronger drink, you can Lebowski it up with a shot of vodka.

¼ cup Kahlúa or other coffee liqueur
1 tablespoon Chocolate Syrup (page 109)
1 tablespoon cream
¾ cup seltzer

In a tall glass, combine the Kahlúa, chocolate syrup, and cream, and stir to thoroughly combine. Top with the seltzer. Gently stir again if needed.

Margarita

YIELD: 1 SERVING

I like margaritas with salt, but a salt-rimmed glass usually results in a couple of sips that are too salty. Incorporating salt directly into the syrup results in a margarita with a nice hint of salt in every sip.

¼ cup tequila
2 tablespoons Cointreau or other triple sec
1 tablespoon Sea Salt–Lime Syrup (page 44)
¼ cup seltzer
Lime wedge, for garnish

In a cocktail shaker, combine the tequila, Cointreau or triple sec, and Sea Salt–Lime Syrup, and shake vigorously. Strain into a glass over ice. Top with the seltzer, and garnish with a lime wedge.

Prickly Pear Margarita

YIELD: 1 SERVING

Prickly pear has a color and flavor that seem like nature designed it with cocktails in mind. In the southwest, it's been used that way since at least the nineteenth century. Tequila is the most natural match for this desert fruit.

⅓ cup tequila
2 tablespoons Prickly Pear Syrup (page 78)
1 tablespoon freshly squeezed lime juice
Ice, as needed
⅓ cup seltzer
Lime wedge, for garnish

In a cocktail shaker, combine the tequila, prickly pear syrup, and lime juice, and shake vigorously. Strain into a glass over ice. Top with the seltzer, and garnish with a lime wedge.

Fizzy Bloody Mary

YIELD: 1 SERVING

Everyone's favorite hangover cure is enhanced with a bit of fizz—perfect for brunch. Everyone likes their Bloodies a little different, so feel free to adjust the recipe as you see fit.

½ cup Tomato Water (page 81)

¼ cup vodka

1 tablespoon freshly squeezed lemon juice

⅛ teaspoon Worcestershire sauce

2 dashes hot sauce

⅛ teaspoon horseradish (optional)

Ice, as needed

¼ cup seltzer

Celery stick, for garnish (optional)

In a cocktail shaker, combine the tomato water, vodka, lemon juice, Worcestershire, hot sauce, and horseradish with ice, and shake vigorously. Strain into a glass. Top with the seltzer, and garnish with celery, if desired.

Sparkling Strawberry Cocktail

YIELD: 1 SERVING

Once you get started with them, you'll find that shrubs are a fantastic cocktail ingredient. This is a twist on a classic strawberry cocktail with the addition of balsamic vinegar and seltzer. If you have any on hand, replace the seltzer and agave with sparkling wine for a slightly different flavor.

¼ cup vodka
2 tablespoons Strawberry-Balsamic Shrub (page 97)
½ tablespoon agave nectar
⅓ cup seltzer

In a cocktail shaker, combine the vodka, strawberry-balsamic shrub, and agave nectar with ice and strain into a lowball glass. Top with the seltzer, and briefly stir. Serve.

Ginger-Grapefruit Martini

YIELD: 1 SERVING

I've long been a fan of ginger-flavored drinks, and my husband likes grapefruit drinks, so when I enjoyed a ginger-grapefruit ice cream at a friend's dinner party, I found the inspiration for a cocktail we both would love.

⅓ cup gin
1 tablespoon Grapefruit Syrup (page 72)
1 tablespoon Ginger Syrup (page 27)
¼ cup seltzer

In a cocktail shaker, combine the gin, grapefruit syrup, and ginger syrup with ice, and shake vigorously. Strain into a martini glass. Top with seltzer, and serve.

Creamy Piña Colada

YIELD: 1 SERVING

Even in the cold of winter, a piña colada can transport you to a tropical beach (or maybe that's just the rum talking).

1 tablespoon Pineapple Syrup (page 76)

¼ cup rum

¼ cup coconut milk, shaken well

½ cup seltzer

In a large glass, stir together the pineapple syrup, rum, and coconut milk to combine. Top with the seltzer, stir, and serve.

Apple Cider Rum

YIELD: 1 SERVING

A great drink to enjoy on a crisp autumn weekend, the rum pairs perfectly with the apple cider's mulling spices.

> 1 tablespoon Apple Cider Syrup (page 71)
> ¼ cup gold rum
> Ice, as needed
> ½ cup seltzer

In a lowball glass, stir together the syrup and rum to combine. Add the ice and top with seltzer, gently stirring again. Serve.

Appendix

Seasonal Soda Making

When harnessing the flavor from fruits, seasonal ones will have the best taste. While these sodas can be made year-round, their flavor will be more vibrant when made in season. Here's a guide to follow.

Spring/Early Summer

Cherry-Almond Syrup (page 65)
Kiwi-Strawberry Syrup (page 60)
Rhubarb-Basil Syrup (page 37)
Rhubarb-Grapefruit Syrup (page 77)
Strawberry-Balsamic Shrub (page 97)
Strawberry Syrup (page 55)

Mid-Summer/Late Summer

Blackberry-Lavender Syrup (page 58)
Blueberry-Lime Syrup (page 61)
Fizzy Cantaloupe Agua Fresca (page 87)
Fizzy Cucumber-Mint Agua Fresca (page 90)
Fizzy Honeydew-Strawberry Agua Fresca (page 92)
Mango-Chile Syrup (page 49)
Mixed Berry Syrup (page 68)
Peach Syrup (page 73)
Plum Shrub (page 94)
Plum-Vanilla Syrup (page 51)
Riesling-Raspberry Syrup (page 61)

Conversions

MEASURE	EQUIVALENT	METRIC
1 teaspoon	--	5 milliliters
1 tablespoon	3 teaspoons	14.8 milliliters
1 cup	16 tablespoons	236.8 milliliters
1 pint	2 cups	473.6 milliliters
1 quart	4 cups	947.2 milliliters
1 liter	4 cups + 3½ tablespoons	1000 milliliters
1 ounce (dry)	2 tablespoons	28.35 grams
1 pound	16 ounces	453.49 grams
2.21 pounds	35.3 ounces	1 kilogram
325°F/350°F/375°F	--	165°C/177°C/190°C

Acknowledgments

Thanks to the fabulous crew at Ulysses Press, most especially my editor, Lauren Harrison, who was a pleasure to work with as she applied all the finishing touches.

About the Author

Andrea Lynn is a food writer and recipe developer with a culinary arts degree from the Institute of Culinary Education. She has over a decade of experience as a writer and editor, including a multiyear stint as Senior Editor at *Chile Pepper* magazine. She continues to write and develop recipes for *Chile Pepper*, as well as the James Beard award–winning website *Serious Eats*. Andrea has worked in the kitchen of a three-star restaurant, as a personal chef, and as a culinary consultant. She is the author of *The I Love Trader Joe's College Cookbook* and *Fresh and Healthy DASH Diet Cooking*. Andrea lives in Astoria, New York. More information about Andrea is available at www.andrealynnfoodwriter.com.